SELF-PORTRAIT

WITH

CEPHALOPOD

T0126106

SELF-PORTRAIT

WITH

CEPHALOPOD

poems

KATHRYN SMITH

Jake Adam York Prize | Selected by francine j. harris

MILKWEED EDITIONS

Published 2021 by Milkweed Editions
Printed in Canada
Cover design by Mary Austin Speaker
Cover art by Mandy Barker
21 22 23 24 25 5 4 3 2 1
First Edition

Milkweed Editions, an independent nonprofit publisher, gratefully acknowledges sustaining support from our Board of Directors; the Alan B. Slifka Foundation and its president, Riva Ariella Ritvo-Slifka; the Amazon Literary Partnership; the Ballard Spahr Foundation; *Copper Nickel*; the McKnight Foundation; the National Endowment for the Arts; the National Poetry Series; the Target Foundation; and other generous contributions from foundations, corporations, and individuals. Also, this activity is made possible by the voters of Minnesota through a Minnesota State Arts Board Operating Support grant, thanks to a legislative appropriation from the arts and cultural heritage fund. For a full listing of Milkweed Editions supporters, please visit milkweed.org.

Library of Congress Cataloging-in-Publication Data

Names: Smith, Kathryn, 1977- author.
Title: Self-portrait with cephalopod : poems / Kathryn Smith.
Description: First edition. | Minneapolis, Minnesota : Milkweed Editions, 2021. | Summary: "Self-Portrait with Cephalopod was selected by Francine J. Harris as the 2019-2020 winner of the Jake Adam York Prize"-- Provided by publisher.
Identifiers: LCCN 2020028615 (print) | LCCN 2020028616 (ebook) | ISBN 9781571315175 (paperback ; acid-free paper) | ISBN 9781571317483 (ebook)

Subjects: LCGFT: Poetry.
Classification: LCC PS3619.M58927 S45 2021 (print) | LCC PS3619.M58927 (ebook) | DDC 811/.6--dc23
LC record available at https://lccn.loc.gov/2020028615
LC ebook record available at https://lccn.loc.gov/2020028616

Milkweed Editions is committed to ecological stewardship. We strive to align our book production practices with this principle, and to reduce the impact of our operations in the environment. We are a member of the Green Press Initiative, a nonprofit coalition of publishers, manufacturers, and authors working to protect the world's endangered forests and conserve natural resources. *Self-Portrait with Cephalopod* was printed on acid-free 100% postconsumer-waste paper by Friesens Corporation.

Contents

You
could die out there. You
could live forever.

TESS GALLAGHER

Ode to Super Friends and Nature Television

Days when the planet seems particularly poised
for disaster, I wear both my cephalopod T-shirt
and my cephalopod ring. Have you heard of a more

Anthropocene coping mechanism? I do it
for the birds with nowhere to land at the critical
point in their migration, for the skewed seasons

and the jungle ants with parasite-skewered brains.
Cave dwellers evolve to survive their sealed-over eyes.
Who needs eyes on a planet wobbling its axis

like a Tilt-A-Whirl? No wonder I wake
motion sick, the fact of death and the ocean and
the mouthparts of insects brimming the list of things

I can't control. Wonder Twin powers, activate!
Form of a fang, a blood-thirsty proboscis,
a tidal turnaround. I wear pants the color of a sea

cucumber, wash my octopus shirt on the saltwater setting.
Anything to understand the universe's categories.
Bats aren't birds, but they're winged. Still life and stillbirth

sound like they'd mean the same thing, but they don't.
Mammals are peculiar, our young feeding on us. Humans
are more peculiar yet, building intricate reefs of plastic

and dread. The beauty of birds isn't flight. It's how they let
their young cram pointy beaks down their throats.
On a planet poised for disaster, I track my desires

in a bullet journal, cover my mammary glands
with a boneless bioluminescence. Delicate dangers
of life in the wild dominate my queue. I watch a robin

side-eye me with its bird face, asking what I did
with its family. I've never been good at discerning
the joyful cries of children at play from the backyard

yowl of a cat fight. If I weren't such a creature of habit,
I'd be a creature of soil, tunneling a nest that writhes
the earth's surface. I am sixty percent water and less than one

percent salt, and when ocean levels rise enough to wash us
from our perches, I'll have zero control over my need
to breathe air, which is not in my control to begin with.

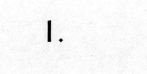

I.

Creation Myth

And the Lord said let ants be fed
from the egg caps of walking stick
insects that hatch disguised as ants.
Let impostors pass undetected
from a subterranean nest. Let fur-bound
beasts carry exoskeletal beasts from one
hinged continent to another, and let land-
bridges break. Let humans break land
and build bridges from elements dug
from the land. Let rats unhinge ribs
from spines and climb through pipes
invented by humans to keep our
shit and nakedness away from
the shit and nakedness of rats.
Let humans set poisoned traps.
And thus I tell you: An erroneous vision
of heaven and hell shall come to you
in books, and this will divide you.
Some will say it's possible
for a child to die and come back
from death having seen the realm
of God. But some will say what
does it matter when earth is a lonely
chasm where children die unnoticed as
we sharpen our knives and whiten
our teeth and tighten our skin and
implore our screens to refresh.

Dumb Beasts

It is difficult to die or we die
too easily, stepping into traffic, letting

cancers consume our bones. This morning,
news of someone famous. We're so sad

for someone we didn't know; we're worth
what the world sees and not what we hide.

At the bus stop, Larry points to a squirrel
flattened in the street. "I hate to see that,"

he says. What can we do? Something dies
every minute—beasts by the hundreds

while we're searching the discography
of the famous departed.

Larry's worked the same job fifty years
and never missed a day. Now

that he's pointed out the dead squirrel,
I can't stop looking at it.

Poem for Trending Tragedy

I am trying to think about the circus collapse.
I am trying to think about the kidnapped
schoolgirls, the extremist who says
they're his for the selling. I am trying, but celebrity
overrides: Look, the young country star
held at gunpoint. Look, the Instagram
argument, the lip-sync fiasco. Someone else
is talking. Someone other than who
we thought. Not who ought. I am trying
to speak about the convict whose execution
went wrong, to parse the name of the chemical
cocktail, to recall the names
of the dead. I know what I know
changes nothing. It augurs
nothing—not when the plague, it turns out,
was not the plague, and we know this now, and not
when the skull on the ocean floor holds tens
of thousands of years of answers. The mouse
that scurries the floorboards could be an old mouse
rejuvenated by a younger mouse's blood, only
to meet the trap. I am trying to remember
those miners in Chile, caught miles below
the ground, but first I must set my mind on things
above, turn my eyes to the clouds (the whence
from which my help comes), the internet sky I am told
will shelter me from collapse. How many days
were they down there? How many miles?
It seems longer now, deeper.
Years and light years. Imagine the researcher's
proposal, his own doubt as he pondered
the tiny needle, as he coined the phrase
mouse transfusion. He'd have to ignore so

many skeptics, spend so many years paying attention
to small creatures, letting the world flicker past,
world beset with wars, world too
impatient for war, world too impatient
for what endures.

Photos of Pig That Appears to Have Blue Fat Beneath Skin Shared on Social Media

O wildest blue. O wild
boar scalpeled
open, peeled back, let me
click you. Let me
like until your blue
fat glows. O phenomenal
mystery, you're so
bright already, o terrible
terrific, shot dead
so someone could
snapshot you. O
shareable beast,
o trending freak
animal, the internet wants
to know if I want
to know more, and how
could I not want
to know more about
pig's blue innards,
to see in the photographs
a bloody hand holding back
the skin. I want
to press my pink finger against
your marbled blue
bubblegum fat.
Oh, how I want that hand
to be my hand.
O swine, how you
bait me, and I cannot
touch you, I can only
click. O pig that appears, I

am also blue, and though
my shade is more
metaphorical, it's like
you know me, and the internet,
it knows me, it says
recommended for you:

Dear Sirs

I am familiar with the traditional forms of revelation:
interpretable dream, flashes of light. But I wonder: What
are some of the modern forms? And do these
Biblical-atmospheric phenomena sometimes
mean nothing?

Last night, for example,
I dreamed a long list of names I was meant
to memorize, then woke to learn a nearby orchard town
had been obliterated by fire.

Is it my cosmic task to remember
who's living and who's lost?
Any insight you can provide
would be appreciated, for until
I know, I fear that fire

will burn the insides of my eyes,
flames licking the wounds and disappearing
names of the dead.

Do You Want to See More?

Our outer-space photos confirm water on Mars. Maybe not now, but at some point in the past. Either way, this comes as a relief, considering our whales have been swimming upriver, captured on drone camera footage. Not the same cameras we sent to Mars, but they could be. There could be whales on Mars. We could send our whales there, pilot whales, pilotless drones, Mars in relief, a planet of lakes and rivers flowing the whole Martian year. When Martian salmon spawn, the red tug of renewal pulls them upstream. Our whales are (d)evolving into salmon. All to the chordate root. Maybe on Mars, the past is the future. The rover's name is Curiosity. The whale's name is Doomed.

Job Qualifications

You must be able, each day, to repeat yourself
a dozen times, a thousand. Each name
must be written in the same shade of ink, the same
slant and heft of hand. It goes without saying you will know
every alphabet forward and back; also the commandments
and their implications and how they are ranked in the various
faith traditions. If the glare of a blank margin
unsettles you, if you grow curious over birthright or cause
of death or are unable to keep your opinions to yourself,
this position is not for you. Our establishment
values discretion and an ability to forget a face even
while you're looking at it. There is no room for error.
We prefer you live alone.

There Are So Many Ways to Decide What to Kill and What to Rescue

But mostly we act on instinct, pluck
predator from prey. *Do ants eat worms?*

the boy asks, and I say, *Sometimes, if the worm
is already dying.* He tells the ants *No*, pries

their sectioned bodies from the writhing
thing. I don't ask how he chose which life

to destroy and which to defend, or tell him
the worm will die anyway. It's our nature

to save what can't be saved. He winces
at a bit of exoskeleton caught beneath

a fingernail, a momentary twinge
sure to loosen in the water when his mother

bathes him before tucking him into bed.

"That's Like the Oldest Trick in the Book, Next to Putting a File in the Cake"

The celebrities trending this smoke-clogged August are B-list at best. But release the police report, and everyone knows who they are. I want to lock myself in my room and never go outside. Lately the sky is the color of dust or mud or toxic sludge or a bruise that's fading or a bruise you want to hide. Who doesn't love celebrity trends? Here's what's hot now: famous name atop a court document, names of minors redacted. Maybe we could just stop talking. Yesterday, a man tied 21 bedsheets together and dangled them from his eighth-floor cell window at the county jail. He'd hired a hitman to kill a business investor just blocks from where I live. I use it as a landmark: *Go past the murder-for-hire house and turn left at the stop sign.* Sky the color of a flood-bloated river. Crime is easier to joke about when we leave the children out of it, when it's just greed and fraud and shale oil. North Dakota is kind of a joke all by itself, how it's suddenly somewhere because that's where the money is. *The accountability of the sheets, that's something we would absolutely increase,* the jail commander said. What a fuck-up. What a fucking joke. I'm scouring the internet for more. Sky the color of sickness. Color of mistake. We're under a state of emergency, what these fires are doing to us. There's no way he could have fit out that window, so it's hard to know what he was thinking. It's as though the children don't have names. The inmates are all accounted for. The celebrity's fame fattens by the second. Wildfire in every direction, and the sky the color of sky, because this is how we live now.

Today is the Day

I will stand shirtless before the machine as it compresses
each breast between two plates, my reward for turning forty.

My God, it's hot out, and I have to walk the ten blocks
to the imaging center without antiperspirant so that no

errant metal seeping through the permeable membrane
we call skin can skew the image or expose my vulnerable tissues

to additional unknown risk. Smoke from distant wildfires
has been clinging to the sky for days now. I think I want

to stop breathing. Blinking, too. This morning I washed
with water siphoned from my neighbor, transported by a hose

linking my house to hers because someone from the City
dug a hole in my yard and closed the valve. *But I haven't showered,*

I thought, as though that mattered more than a foundation's
seeping cracks. I know a leaking pipe in August is basically

a faucet left running in a drought. Imagine the cancers
I will hypothetically absorb today: aluminum leaching

toward my breasts, chemicals finding my pores
as water bounces off my skin, airborne particulates

landing on the sponge of my lungs. Today is the day,
and yesterday, and tomorrow. It'll be a while before

the planet dies, and meanwhile, we have to live here.
Let's all make ourselves comfortable while we can is one way

to argue this inevitability. *Let's sit in the stench of our bodies*
for the sake of the children, whose stinking bodies need a planet

to sit on, too, is another. What camp I'm in changes daily,
sometimes by the hour. Why do mammograms make me

contemplate apocalypse? The end will come at us
like an uncomfortable procedure that exists to detect

dangers brought on by other dangers we do nothing
to quell. Mostly I'm resigned to it, doing what I can

when it suits me. It's too hot and smoky to walk,
so my friend is letting me borrow her Prius.

Regarding the Advertised Position

Dear Anyone:

For some time now, I've fancied myself
a list-maker:
>Monarchs and their successors in Babylonian kingdoms
>What to do in a garden in February
>Things of which nothing new can be said

and I can forward you any one of these lists upon request.

As you can see from this letter, my handwriting
is immaculate, my spelling excellent, and I excel
at all things alphabetical, bibliographical, celestial, divine,
etc. As for specific experience, I have recently, to hone
my objectivity, stopped observing. I don't remember
the sound of snowmelt dripping from a roof, the gleam of icicles'
sharp translucence. Sunrise and sunset, of course,
forgotten. Their colors: gray. The smell
of wood smoke on a winter night the same
to me as a new-mown field in spring. This skill,
I believe, will keep me from judgment. Daylight
or moonlight, whatever this is, if I stepped outside now
I'd be lost on the only road home.

2.

Spell to Turn the World Around

Begin each day collecting birds battered
in the night by creatures bent on malice.
Give thanks for dew and viscera's bright litter,
leaves brought down by drought and feathers damp

with blood. When you say you love fall, be sure
you know it's death's season. Take shallow
breaths, reminding you of summer's smoke,
a wildfire bruise that locked us all inside.

Cling to warm October afternoons
as vow to live a waterless winter.
Drive cross-state to the firefighter's grave
and read the poem he memorized at seventeen,

three years before flames overtook the vehicle
he rode in, trying to reach disaster.

Psalm Formula: Anti-epistle

It is said in God
there is no darkness.
It is also said
I am made
in God's image.
Never shadow, never
afterimage, not
the every-color opposite
of the photo negative.
I am fearfully and wonderfully
made, made wonderfully
fearful. When I
was a child, I acted
like a child.
When I was afraid,
I acted afraid.
Put these things
away. Surely goodness
will dog me all the days
of my life. Mercy
will clip
my heels.
I will dwell
in the house of the Lord,
where no one wakes
on the wrong side
of dreaming,
where the tables
are all overturned.

The Windows Kept On

I.

That year, whole seasons collapsed
around us. We were shirt-sleeved and suddenly
pummeled by storm. I prayed to be kept
fog-encased and unaccountable, out
of morning's throat. Days began with dogs
circling the pre-dawn gray. Circling, like
they knew how much we repeated. The windows
kept on with their illusions of rain. My dreams
were noisy and always the same, clouds
bruising us into earth. Drilling us like seed
into saturated furrows, certain to rot.

II.

According to the book, every dream means
fear of death. Even when I'm inappropriately
kissed—one night on the mouth, another on the soft
of my breast, through the shirt. Nothing more
than tenderness. Another night I witness rebirth, strange
and apocalyptic: A human in miniature writhes
and contorts its face before a bird breaks through
its belly, fully feathered coverts rising Phoenix-like
from its ruptured center. Surely this will kill it, small
genderless Adam, ribcage transformed to phalanx
of wing. What wakes me isn't the dying, or even the being
born. It's the muffled cry of animals confused by light.

Cast Your Cares Upon Him

*A 25-year-old woman told a witness Saturday she
threw her 15-month-old son down 50 feet of a river
embankment because the devil told her to do it,
according to court documents.*
—THE SPOKESMAN-REVIEW

Are we fish or birds? If we are born
gilled, then surely a winged rebirth awaits us,

no longer earthbound, our animal
slits sealed over, sealing out
knowledge of what
came before. The people who grew from fish

do not remember life in water, the memory
of it shed with that life's scales. So hail
mammalian, for we are people now,
upright, prisoners to our limbs. Who can blame,

then, the young mother who tossed her child
down the embankment so he would know this world

is pain and pain again, is grit and scab. Is
gristle. Is obeying another's voice. Is being forced
to throw what we love most to the river and watching him
hit rock. No wings, no fins. Only dust.
She wanted him to remember

what it's like to breathe
inside something else, that world-before-the-
world of the womb. That space where
being trapped is the only way we stay alive.

Chronic and Nameless

The cat is dying—though I know we all are, since the day we're born or before that, when we're that cell-knot of embryo, that hoped-for thing or mistake. But the cat is dying more so than usual, and I have become a person who follows a cat around the house with a handkerchief, hoping to catch the strings of snot that trail so pitifully from his nostrils since cats can't say what they need. *And they* hate *to breathe through their mouths*, the veterinarian says, and she emphasizes the word *hate* the way preteen girls do when discussing their morphing bodies. In fifth grade we all wanted to be veterinarians, but by sixth we were over it and planning our pop-star careers. *Discovered so young,* the magazines would say. By then we'd learned something about animals, but nothing about death, except that sometimes a father will leave a note that reads *I didn't think any of you loved me anymore,* which they'll find with him at the beach cabin, the tide outside receding before it comes in.

What Spoils in the Sun

You'd think by now I'd stop asking what's wrong with me
that I sleep so much. You'd think the chickens would stop
complaining from their coop. I pick tomatoes:
sauce tomatoes and beefsteaks and tomatoes especially
for drying. Each ripens in its own time,
though they all set at once. I push up my sleeves.
I've got this wedding to go to and I want my shoulders
evenly burned in my sleeveless dress.
What's wrong with me? I swallow coffee, ibuprofen.
I toss the chickens a bitter cucumber. You'd think
they'd stop complaining. I thought I was done
with weddings. For years I spent my summers
sitting through them, and then they stopped and then
the babies. What's wrong with me
that I don't like weddings? It must be all that
happiness. Who needs so many goddamned tomatoes?
Calabash and Jaune Flame and Bread & Salt.
Who could resist such names? I suppose that's why
some people have babies, to name something and call it
by name and have it answer. At first I named the chickens,
but when they started dying, I took to calling them all Bird.
My neighbor says, "Hi, girls!" as though they're children
when she calls to them over the fence, tossing them melon rinds
and overgrown zucchinis they peck at briefly, then leave to rot.

Psalm Formula: Of One Afflicted

File under: Bad days. Attributed to:
a) fate; b) chance; c) divine plan; d) other.
Explain mathematics to tragedy. Explain death
to those who go on living.

> (What good
> is butter without bread? An umbrella without
> the storm? We must long for pain
> to pray as we do, to a god who shapes it so
> fearfully and wonderfully.)

      File under:
Misinterpretations. Lack of understanding. No long-
term vision.

> (The lamb
> laid down with the lion, and the lion
> tore it open. Praise
> and lament are overlapping again.)

In conclusion: My ways are not your ways.

> (The birds of sorrow are carrion feeders.)

Because you fashioned such an awful day,
I love you. Because I have suffered, I believe.

Like Humans

Rats live in attics and cellars. Bats live in towers and caves. Rats and bats, bats and rats. A snarled mess of hair is a rats' nest. A bat in the belfry is a metaphor for crazy. A rats' nest is also a crammed-full house, and hoarders are said to have bats in the belfry. They're pack rats. They're batty. I'm a little crazy myself, which is to say my brain needs help blocking the reuptake of serotonin and norepinephrine. I'm fine now. It's fine. Bats and rats both thrive in filth and darkness. Bats and rats, rats and bats. Both suckle young at the teat. Born helpless, like humans. There's a syndrome eroding bats' skin at the muzzle. Deterioration of wing. Abnormal activity in the daytime. I used to lie awake at night, sleep till noon. I'm fine now. It's fine. Six percent of bats carry rabies. Rats carry hantavirus and rat-bite fever, tularemia and plague. They carry disease like a message. Humans with rabies go crazy. Bats can survive it. White-nose syndrome spreads through caves, infecting bats as they hibernate. The air carries disease like a message, and the bats cannot escape.

Waking Late to a Late Spring

The wind did not wake me—not when it tore
the fence down, not when it rattled maple trees
that grew thick with leaves while I slept. Now the sun
presses past the roofline, hunted by thunder. Now birds

fill the mud-addled yard, pulling fat grubs
from the weeds. Dear wrecker
in the ruin, dear great keeper of forecasts
and dust: I know what spring should be:

Worms tangled in their androgynous trysts,
spider webs strung from branch to power line,
hopeful and extravagant. This season's all
storms and shade. I hear how close

the rain is. There's nothing I can do.

Parable of the Sower

Preacher says the seed falls
where the sower casts it, sometimes
to the wrong soil. We can't know
why the sower has done this: half a lifetime
feeling fallow, nearly past hope. I pray God
counts the days until my point
of breaking, confident
in his calculations. Lord, make me
a textbook example: catchweed matted
into some rough animal, carried miles
before the barbs let go. Maybe
the wind will be enough to
release me. Maybe salvation
is in the death of the beast.

Concerning Nectar, Concerning Brack

The day's so bright it's bleached
monochromatic. We're dressed
in gray to match what's left. The news
is just noise, and we long to dwell
inside it—anything but this stark

provision, everything sour: coffee
the shade of brackwater, last year's

gooseberry jam. This bread
smarts the tongue. A stomach-flip
out of dreaming. Not even birds
find sweetness—only water

stained red. We've omitted
sugar hoping to slow invisibly
quick wings, to glimpse
the proof of flying, green flutter

altered to simple mechanics. Soon
the hummingbirds will abandon the feeder,
its false nectar, and no kindness
we can offer will lure them back.

Cracking the Egg

I scramble the egg
until it does not resemble
egg—no longer the globe

a body bore into
the world for a purpose
entirely other. First I scraped

the blood-knot
from the albumen—trace
of its potential, of what

reminds me of me,
life force hidden
in the viscous clot.

When the speckled hen
grew listless and drew her head
to her puffed chest,

I quarantined her
in a crate lined with soft
clean shavings

where she could suffer alone.
Two days later, when I entered
the dark garage,

her carcass, as she stiffened,
had pushed through the crate's
makeshift door

as though she'd tried for escape.
Her eyelids made a final
translucent seal.

It was like
scooping a dead wasp
from a windowsill or

freeing a bloodied mouse
from a sprung trap
as I lifted her body

into a plastic garbage sack
and placed it
in the trash: *So much*

for that one. Not loss
exactly, but more notice
than I give the ova that slip

unceremoniously from
my body when the moon
shifts from sliver

to smudge, simply
doing away
with what there's nothing

to be done with. I
have seen the self's
raw resemblance

wriggling with need
in dreams
where she's

a misplaced parcel,
wrapped and left
in a bureau drawer.

She's large-headed
and adult-voiced,
and when

I wake, it's with
such relief to be
alone with morning, which

demands enough,
the way it
repeats itself, its hunger.

Meditation Among the Fragments

Some mornings pray themselves open.
I skirt the shoreline, weaving with the tide,

my pockets heavy
with rocks and shells, ancient

litter, evidence of a life
lived at the edges of things. Some pieces

are only ever
broken, bone pores gritted

with mica, wave-smoothed rift
and algal stain. This sand-

dollar fragment chips from its star-whorl,
vulnerable there, where beauty

meets function meets beauty. I press a hand against
my own center, feel

the seam where waves would crack me. In such a vast
calcifying tumbler, who could keep

what's necessary? I let silt and
silver wash through my foothold. Finger

the grit. Let the tide, as it
will, draw in.

3.

The Danger

It was the saddest day of our lives: the day we learned
the new eighth grade homeroom teacher
had driven through the South Shore Road guardrail

two weeks into the school year. I don't remember
her name—Miss Something, Miss Not-
From-Around-Here. But even so, it was sad—the saddest

we'd ever been, even those of us
in Mrs. Jones' class across the hall who'd barely seen
Miss So-and-So's face but whose friends

could swear she was young, and she was so nice,
and pretty, maybe, as they usually are,
and new to our town where the roads

curve without warning. Poor Miss What's-Her-Name, born
without our compass, without the maps
that live inside you if you're raised here, furrowing

a hairline or veining a varicose thigh. Poor Miss No-
Longer-With-Us: She was only trying to learn the danger
the rest of us can't seem to shake. And poor us, poor

young survivors, thirteen and teacherless and not
the ones flung through the rain-slicked windshield
to the vast and glittering lake.

Independence Day

We grew up believing in cold heat.
Summer days sank to the lake's dark shiver.

All the girls on the dock pretended it didn't
sting, the gasp of regret as the body

breaks the surface. I would have taken
a photograph, but I wanted the chance

to remember things differently—no sunlight
cleaving into us the way it did, no faces

unrecognizably shadowed. Once you hit
water, nothing was the same. It was

See you next year and *Stop by on the 4th*. It was
shoulders burnt to blister. Never kisses. I ached

for a bathing suit's just-so pucker, a glimpse
of goosefleshed glisten. Barbecue smoke

and fireworks clouded twilight
with particulate burn, acrid and unforgiving.

In that tear-inducing suspension, the sulfured air
souring my lungs kept me breathing.

Self-Portrait with Cephalopod and Digitalis Purpurea

for Maya

Sometimes a girl doesn't need a reason to place
a foxglove blossom on her tongue. It's enough
to like the idea that the heart could stop because
of flowers. It's that or be crushed like ichthyosaurus
in a kraken's grasp by my own sadness, fossilized
in unnatural linear patterns, finally measured
by the geometry of loss. I don't need another reason
to fear the ocean; I already know it could swallow me
from the inside if I tried to breathe it in. Everything
beautiful is dangerous, and attempting beauty's
a risk, like the dress my mom's friend made me
for the eighth-grade dance. So often, things don't
hang together the way I imagine. That seafoam bow
over my pale, scant breasts looked nothing
like the pattern promised. It made my head hurt,
knowing how little meets our expectations,
so I refused the last dance and my date left
without me. He spent the next four years
pretending I wasn't there, my shadow
scuttling the halls of the high school beside him.
Sometimes a girl doesn't need a reason to want
to disappear behind the unseen framework
of collarbones. I think mine would look lovely
in a cephalopod's garden after she had spit away
the sateen straps. Have you ever wondered
what's beneath the skin, working? I know
so little, I wouldn't recognize my own heart if I saw it
outside my body. I wouldn't know my own bones

arranged in an ocean bed, an octopus coaxing
them to root in the sea floor until their stalks
grew thick with mouthlike blooms.

Sulfur

You can fool a man, but not a machine. When the
machine is willful, you have to find out why.
—JOHAN RICHTER

Johan Richter had a vision: a machine that never
sleeps, digesting wood chips ad infinitum, steam and salt
and sodium sulfide breaking cellulose down to its elemental
self in the very model of efficiency. The resulting product,
thanks to Richter, would never be inconsistent. No more
would the white plumes rising from the waterfront mill
cease. I was nine years old and already staring down a horizon
that continually manufactured clouds. Thank Johan Richter
for the sky's perpetuity, the sulfurous air I breathed
as I pedaled the neighborhood. Thank him for the machinery
my father oiled at any necessary hour to ensure the digester's
endless chugging. For swing shifts and graveyard shifts, my sister
crying when he left for the mill, not knowing when
she'd see him. Thank Richter for work, and for lack of work,
for union strikes and layoffs. For the first move, and the second.
Thank him for fooling us. The devil, as they say, is in
the details: Sulfur's another word for brimstone, that belching
hell-stench so many preachers slam their fists over. But thanks
to Johan Richter, we know better. We know the god
is in the machine and necessity is the mother of invention.
Consider the Taoists. In their search for a potion to achieve
immortality, they concocted instead an explosive powder
that revolutionized the face of war. Technology
spreads quickly, even when it's born of irony.
It's in our chemical make-up, in the sulfur we all hold
in our bodies—more than the oceans hold, more
than the Earth's crust, though it shifts and shrugs
and spews its brimstone fireworks skyward. Every beauty

is a byproduct of danger. Water seeps beneath the surface
and bubbles up again, warmed by minerals and sulfur,
in the hot springs that soothed my mother's prearthritic
joints, before the real deterioration set in. Johan Richter
can't really be blamed. Surely he never imagined we'd see
an end to these trees, or find another way to carry what's
necessary. There's such a smooth reliability to paper. Our sacks
filled with hot dog buns and Styrofoam cups, we'd hike a mile
into the forest and sit in the hot springs' mud, before someone
found a way to redirect the healing waters closer to the road,
built pools encased in concrete, and pumped the water
in. They thought it more civilized, though despite
the locker rooms and showers to scrub our skin and hair,
we still went home smelling like something rotten.

The Young Eat What These Birds Disgorge
from Their Crops

Old World vultures track their prey by vision. New World vultures
smell the dead a mile away. Drawn to decay. Oh, to be so

unambiguously guided. I want to lie down in the battlefield
and be scavenged. My mother wants to know who fought

the battle. She's from the Old World. We drive a corkscrew road
while vultures churn the sky. History repeats itself. I keep waiting

for the world to turn around. From atop the butte, we see every
direction, miles of acres of nonnative wheat. The Old World

sighs, *Well, we lost the battle*. I hem and mumble, haw and lie.
The New World spreads its New-World wings. I zip my coat

against a wind that whistles through vulture feathers, alerts
the wake to feeding time. History defeats itself. I want the sky

to stutter above me, spitting down its gawk and cry.
Different species of vulture eat different parts of the carcass,

some dropping bones from high above, exposing the marrow
of what's killed by something else. Without decomposers, the dead

would clutter the earth. Vultures circle, necklacing our errors.
I want the descent—the swoop and pluck, clear to my sharp

and nationless bones. The earth turns, or it doesn't, we spiral
back down, and the vultures overhead wait for something to die.

All God's Creatures Got a Place in the Choir

Who resigned the rabbit to such blinking
silence when squirrels are given a stridency
that overwhelms the stuttering finch,

drowns the pulse of the worm's twin hearts
undulating the length of its body. The puppy
left chained in the midday heat practices every

tonality of whimper until, far into night, it
yelps itself to sleep. One hundred
roosters, each with one manacled foot,

caw and cry and pry at the chains that keep them
just far enough apart to fend off
violence. From their individual roosts, calculatingly

spaced across a suburban Ohio acre, each bird
answers the call of another. Each day yields
four hours, at most, of silence. Otherwise, the sky

is constant collision, the auditory wreckage of twenty
thousand swallowed reports. Or so
the neighbors say. To the breeder,

it's music, it's beautiful, and for Chrissakes, it's
the country. What's it for if not roosters? What's the wide
world if not a cacophony of interpretation—

the clicking of crickets portending autumn
or plague, the roosters finally asleep when the rabbit's
quiet deception turns the garden to ruin.

And the Shrill Shall Lead the Blind

*Snake-occupied screech owl nests produce more
and healthier fledglings than do snake-free nests.*
—NATIONAL WILDLIFE MAGAZINE

When the mouse lies down with you, you've already
maimed him. The songbird, still warm but without

her voice, has a place in your burrow, borrowed
from the woodpecker who no longer needs it.

Your realm, eastern screech owl, is bloody
survival. It's a headless meal dangling

from a mother's grasp, death brought close.
But a nest lined with what feeds soon festers.

What of your hatchlings' gaping hunger
when parasites quiver your walls? Enter

the snake, blind and coiled alive around the beak
that bears it. Slippery deliverer, she'll devour

the maggots that threaten your young,
unaware of the kingdom they've been born to,

the rules they break when the serpent beds down
with a raptor's nestlings, and both creatures thrive.

Perception

The jersey died on a frosty March morning while my brother and I tried to catch the vapor of each other's frozen breath in our mittens. When our father left the barn, we probed the cow's ears, tried to pry her lips apart, thinking somewhere within her she held the answers to waking and sleeping and death. My brother pressed my hand against one milky eye. I expected give, softness like new cheese, but it was smooth beneath the pads of my fingers, as though a clean sheet of ice held the mystery of sight in place.

From that day on the surface was never enough. I popped the face from the mantel clock, followed honeybees to their hollowed trees, slid my body beneath the scrim of algae sealing the pond. I held my breath as the professor placed a green-tinted orb before me on a glass tray, a sharp smell rising. I steadied my hand, gripped the blade, and scored a clean incision between cornea and sclera. When I pulled the iris from the eye's center, that cow's-eye-view slicked my fingers, and as I held the lens to the light, the world blurred without the shimmering blue membrane still hidden beneath the retina, an iridescent dream exposed only when the eye is empty and formless and coaxed inside-out.

After the Funeral

We pushed our bicycles up to Halstaad's Field, fallow
for years now, overrun with brambles and thistle.
Sweat soaked our clothes, too black for August amid weeks
without rain. At the hill's crest, the farmhouse faded from view—
    mother
at a window somewhere, inconsolably repeating the scripture's
    refrain—
and we cut across to the narrow trail we'd worked three summers
    carving.

It took longer than it should have to catch my breath, but when
    Eddie said,
"I dare you," I mounted my bicycle and let fly. The kingdom of
    heaven
is like a cloudless summer sky, earth beneath it parched
and aching. I could feel Eddie gaining on me, and I pedaled
harder, veins thrumming my temples, reveling in the dust storm
we had created, coating our clothes and our faces. The kingdom is like
the forgotten field, rocks heaved to the surface by centuries of frost.
Then, the scree-strewn clearing a hairsbreadth away, which,
at the point of overtaking, the slightest clip of the handlebars
sends you toward, and over, chain sprung from its wheel, pedals
spinning a windmill fury. The kingdom of heaven is like—*look, Eddie,
no hands!*—rising from the saddle as though lifted, weightless, close
as I've been to birds when their wings are stretched in flight.

When we returned, mother wouldn't know us, transformed
as we were by sweat and dust, beaming like children who'd never
lost a thing, who'd tasted the kingdom's salt moments before
the yawning sky lets go to gravity, before the tumble
and burn, the elusive wisp of freedom snatched by the sear
of gravel as it enters, irrevocably, the flesh.

Revisiting Salt Creek

To know I'm home, I clamber to the farthest point
this bay allows, my hands salt-washed
and stunned with cold. I find where ridges match
my palms, their rigid grooves, the scars I bear
from years spent grasping at these ledges,
skirting cliffs to know their bounds. And this was youth's

solace: to never learn how landing feels,
how it maims. To feel it in the skin
but not the bones—not so deep as that.
A fish leaps, then skims the surface from
beneath, fin rippling water until it finds
the bay. I trace its route toward safety.

I risk high tide's potential stranding
to pocket rocks and shells, these souvenirs.

Psalm Formula: Of the Psalmist

Weeping spends the night, but joy
comes in the morning. Morning
is bitter wind. You are not in the frost-

killed garden.
You are not in the henhouse with birds
too old to lay. Let me be
underwhelmed. Let us analogize:

My dreams are like birds getting by
on what meager scratch winter offers.

My dreams are the horses beggars ride.
They're what's stampeded.
They're the dust
that praises
dust.

4.

Most of Us Aren't Beautiful, Though Some Learn How

The honeysuckle outgrows its trellis
and climbs the weeds. I'm back

where I started: stuck in a parable
I cannot, botanically, and do not,

theologically, believe. I've been gathering
dried pods of sweet peas because I know

I'll need their fragrance come spring.
Flung seeds leave coiled husks

behind, taut as a ringlet my hair
would never hold. Stupid world

with its spilled abundance and magazine
promises and thrift-store curlers. By the end

of the dance, my head looked
slept on, aphids clinging to the wilt

of my homemade corsage. Blessed are
the plain, for they shall come into their own

one day—in a field, most likely, bandanna-
clad, swatting at blackflies, burnt

to the sleeves. See how much
happier I/we/you can be when I/we/you

stop caring? I hardly even want
to die anymore.

Of Gods and Galaxies

The seal would last a billion years
if it had to. Did the hands shake,
placing the copper phonograph
inside, etched with thunderclap
and rock 'n' roll and sixty nuanced
voices saying hello? I was perfect
then, screaming, too small for wrong,
having just been washed of my
invisible sins. As Voyager II
hurtled through the burn, I lay
on my back facing every beyond:
outer atmosphere, ceiling, the mobile
dangling over my crib. The hope:
a being enough like us to understand
our enclosed instructions would pull
the record from its aluminum sleeve
and set the provided needle to our desires.
Was I thinking of the water? There
was so little of it, a trickle, really,
and if I cried, it's because I wanted
more, to float again in amniotic
safety, weightless. There were
nine planets then, bumbling
around a yellow chipboard sun
suspended by a filament
invisible to newborn eyes.

Legends Say

The maps furrow the palm. They vein a varicose thigh. If you'd been born here. If you'd been born. If your father worked graveyard and told your mother, just a few hours' sleep, and he dreamed the saw's whine while she breathed through each contraction. If the maps broke when they stripped her veins and the bleeding wouldn't quit. To squelch or stanch or stop a rock-bound river. To dam the blood and its antibodies, a river's platelets and plated fish. To unbox a collection of antique plates and find hidden there a photograph of your mother holding a child you've never seen, its fish-face gasping. If you'd been born as wood is split, the sawmill crying. If you'd stopped your ears and hadn't heard the foghorn, the ferry horn, the lady of the lake's tragic story. If you'd looked to your palm and chosen another path. If the trails were marked. If the sign read 1,000 miles to nowhere: Head due west.

Inheritance

We're both afraid of the brain
deteriorating before the body

and of swimming, or drowning,
which, to me, seems the same.

When I was small, I was certain
that one day the padded wall

of the elementary school gymnasium
would open to flood the room

with chlorinated water. What
made me believe such a thing

would happen? There's a photograph
of me as an infant crawling straight

for the incoming tide. Somewhere
in the few years between, fear

crept in like an insect, so light
you can't feel it until it bites.

She knows deterioration of the body
already, and the brain fog that follows

like an overprotective parent. Love
is knitted there, in the vessel I will wash

with a damp cloth when she is dying.
Will I? I am not tender, impatient

with requests, though I've been known
to bathe an ailing hen, to shoo ants

intent on thieving grubs from a wasp's
fallen nest. Yesterday, I reached a blind

hand to prize lettuce from its root
and plunged the tip of my index finger

straight into a wasp's stinger. Now
everything I point to is pain. Last time

she called, she asked what she should do
with the stack of music she found

shoved in the hall closet, blooming
with mold. It was her mother's, so she

was sad to lose it, but she didn't know
what she was going to do with it anyway.

When I Stepped on the Mouths of Other Creatures,
I Did Not Apologize

Here, the world strips itself to kelp
teeming with flies. It comforts me,
knowing gulls will pry a locked shell

until it gives. I found a barnacle latched
inside a barnacle's mouth—fastened
to its own kind. I took it home, cradled

in tissue for the journey, then startled
at the sea-stench when I unwrapped it.
I'm a blood cage, the sort of creature

who looks for God when I feel my brain
spin out from my body. I think there's a tree
leafing out in my throat. *I never considered*

what the end of my life would be like,
my grandmother said as I wheeled her
down the corridor. I consider it constantly,

in every cliff where roots strain to hang on,
every chamber spiraled with sand. First
the snail died, then the crab. I offer my finger

to the anemone's blind suckle. I can't
feed anything. The tide carries its living
and its dead together, lets the shore

reveal and retreat. When does the body
become distinct from the mind? We know
the exoskeletal breaks. Clog of leaves.

That word *corridor*—so much worse
than *hallway*. Passage, permanence.
Forsake, forsaken. We blame the ocean,

whether or not the ocean is to blame.

Situs Inversus

As the body develops in utero,
the heart is its first visible asymmetry—
a whirl of cilia around the midline
looping left. But throw the tilt
off-kilter, and the heart begins
somewhere else, spleen and liver
following in a reversal of the internal organs
that's harmless if complete, hidden
beneath a bilateral frame.

//

I was considering the soul
and where it resides and whether
it's like an organ, and if so,
if the body's functioning
requires it, like the heart, lungs,
etc., or if the soul, like the spleen
or the gall bladder or the eyes,
is something the body
can live without.

//

Do you know where your heart is?
Split upon a table, would doctors gasp
to find the spread of viscera inverted?
When I scalpeled the squid, I had to first
locate its mouth to know where
among the tentacled mess
lay its center. I was a child,
and at the end of class, our teacher

tossed the flesh we'd butchered
in flour and fried it in an electric skillet.
It tasted like everything I didn't know
about the world's inner workings,
rubbery and caught between the teeth.

//

I took an internet quiz that said my soul
was shaped like a rhombus, which I found
disappointing in its flatness and lopsided
appearance. Could it really be so simple
as two pair of parallel sides? *Rhombus*
comes from the Greek, meaning a thing
that spins, so I imagine my soul balancing
itself on one of its more acute points and whirling
like a top, dimensional, full of perpetual motion,
navigating the unseen interstices
between the physical and spiritual realms.

//

A squid has three hearts. Its chitinous
beak, so adept at tearing prey, is hard
to break down, swimming in the bellies
of whales with plastic bags and the myth
of Jonah and the ocean's secret knowledge
of unseen beasts. Cephalopods
of a certain size must be tenderized
before cooking. "Pound them
mercilessly on a solid surface,"
The Joy of Cooking directs.
On the first edition's cover,
Martha of Bethany, patron saint of cooks,
housewives, and domestic servants,

conquers an Art Deco dragon
that's spined and scaled and tailed in ways
no kitchen is equipped to tackle.

//

It was 1788 when students of anatomy
opened a cadaver to the first recorded case
of *situs inversus*, the body's every organ properly
formed but flipped along the axial spine
in mirror image of their expectations.
Without scans and research involving fish and mice
and knowledge of embryonic cilia and the vital
angle of their swirling in the flow of what
surrounds them, no one could know
what the body contained until they cut it open.

//

By the time tenth-grade biology assigned the splaying of frogs,
I'd developed a squeamishness disguised
as moral opposition. I scrawled notes as my classmates
scored incisions in reptile flesh. Even now
I grow woozy at my own blood
pooling a wound or the terrified breaths
of an immature squirrel dropped from
the maple's high branches to my driveway.

//

According to the Golden Legend, Martha of Bethany
subdued the beast terrorizing the people of Tarascon
with the flash of a cross and a splash of holy water
before binding it with her girdle. The dragon
was half beast, half fish, horned and winged

and stronger than any known thing,
a creature we cannot, in modern times,
account for, despite our longing
for Nessie and Sasquatch, our knowledge
of saltwater crocs and leatherback turtles.
When Martha first met the Tarasque, as the beast
was called, an unfortunate man dangled from its mouth
in evidence of its savagery. She tamed the beast
and led her convert by its makeshift leash
to the center of town, where the people
tore it to pieces.

//

For squid or octopus, fried, stuffed, casseroled
or simmered in ink sauce, "make sure first
that your victim is dead—by striking it a conclusive
blow to the head." Irma Rombauer's cookbook
assumes that small game has arrived at your kitchen
lifeless. For those, she begins her instruction with steps
for skinning, for which she advises gloves. Snails
are harvested during hibernation. Preparation
of frogs begins with the legs. If turtle
is not purchased tinned, it's best
to box your terrapin for at least a week,
feeding it ground meat and water
until the animal rids itself of all impurity.

//

If everything inside the body lines up
but the heart is in the wrong place,
it's fatal. Sometimes the heart finds the chest's
left side, but the valves and chambers
form a reversal requiring complex surgery

to rearrange. The heart isn't shaped
like its symbol. The soul is a mystery,
lopsided, poised to tumble. After Martha
wrestled the dragon, she spent her life
in constant prayer, subsisting on one meal
each day which never contained the flesh
or milk or eggs of animals—a penance
for how the townspeople slaughtered
the beast she'd meant to save.
I'd like to be a better person. One
whose rhombus soul spins simultaneously
acute and obtuse, without contradiction.
One who is able to kill a maimed squirrel
rather than watch its quick, shocked breaths,
cringing at the small scream it emits when I lift it
from the driveway to a cardboard box I'll set
inside the shed, out of the reach of cats
and other predators, hoping that as night
dips near freezing, death will take
its own course.

Salt-Washed Pictograph Just Beyond the Abandoned Bunker

after Melissa Kwasny

To peel the bark of madrone to its pith. To drive a road grown mossy between tire tracks. To know a place by its guardrails, and where they're fractured, its bridges and those who've jumped. I've grown from these things, then toward them. My ancestors were first to clear-cut these forests, and I must claim this as my history, the way I claim—what? Loneliness? The violence of species toward species, an oil rig's midnight vanishing. Blank harbor. A seagull drops its thieved mussel again and again to crack it open. I claim this exposed meat. These kelp heads bobbing the high tide look almost animal, an orderly procession of sea lions. Peel the bark from red to pale. A person could, if a person wanted to. A person could reach the deepest part.

Tree of Life

To the river whose dam was torn out
one hundred years too late: There is no rapture.
To the dog locked in the closet, left
to die, and to the road-killed eagle: You will not
be spirited away. The earth rebuilds itself
around us. Whether or not we live. Whether
or not we suffer. To twenty-year-old Kala Williams, soaking up
the murky edgewater when they found you: Your rock-
bruised body will still be here when the river
is made new, food
for the roots of the tree
of life growing on either side, out of the snags
exposed when the river finds
a new course, sooner than anyone
expected. This is the revelatory tide, raising all
things up: buried or sunken, casketed
or tarp-wrapped, duct-taped. Zip-tied. This
the kingdom: all flesh
united, the shore revealing what the world
cannot hide. Nothing hides from the river.
It's a short trek from the alley to its scrub-strewn banks.
The perfect disposal site, perfect
resting place. What holds us here
besides a door, latched
and bolted on the other side?
Besides silt and hundred-year-old concrete? Every river
can hold itself back that long, biding. New alder scrub
sprouts its underbrush
to hide us again and all the small living things
seeking shelter, skeletons
of every size. We know what company
we keep, the moonlit alley's capacity for danger, how long

until the dog suffocates or starves. This rocky
existence abrades us all, crying till our breath
runs out, nothing
in our chests but some universe's
inertia, some pulling through of molecules
that rearrange themselves with every shift
and exhalation. Had the eagle not been killed,
it would still be out there, killing. This is the shore
where they found her. The bed she slept in
undisturbed until they drained the lake.
Even this struck bird keeps one wing
raised toward sky. How
quickly the fish return. The tree's new leaves
are glossy. They rustle in the wind.

A Permeable Membrane in the Mutable Cosmos

Tell me again of the lepers who learn
      to shed their disastrous skin
by eating the meat of vipers: something
transmutable in the flesh. The ancients
          spent lifetimes considering
the resurrection of irretrievable
parts:
      wolf-devoured flank, eyes
of martyrs pecked clean in a village square.
             Tell me again
about the new heaven and the new earth,

when the bear returns an unblemished arm
to its faithful socket, when mountains
      open their mouths to receive
conduits and I-beams and engagement diamonds
and the fish ladders the rivers will give up
          with their dams when the earth
is made new.
      Tell me the formula

for feeling whole again
      after tragedy. The equation for how much time
I needed after saying no
      before I'd tell you yes.
Tell me I'll never be alone, even when I want
to be alone.

Notes

"Dumb Beasts" is in direct conversation with Maya Jewell Zeller's poem "A Small Replica of History" and owes its title to that poem.

"Poem for Trending Tragedy" received the Allied Arts Foundation Poetry Award in 2019. Thank you to Keetje Kuipers for selecting it.

"Do You Want to See More?" owes its form and its final line to Ellen Welcker's poem "It's Called the Sea," published in her collection *Ram Hands.*

"That's Like the Oldest Trick in the Book, Next to Putting a File in the Cake" takes its title, as well as the italicized line attributed to the jail commander, from an Aug. 21, 2015, article in *The Spokesman-Review* newspaper regarding an escape attempt at the Spokane County Jail.

"Today is the Day" owes a debt of gratitude to Laura Read, for letting me borrow her Prius.

"Self-Portrait with Cephalopod and Digitalis Purpurea" owes a debt to Maya Jewell Zeller's poem "Foxglove," from her collection *Rust Fish,* and owes its existence to our poetic conversations.

"All God's Creatures Got a Place in the Choir" references the PBS documentary *The Natural History of the Chicken.* Thank you to Adrian Rogers for introducing me to this film.

"Perception" is after Linda Bierds' poem "Windows," from her book *The Ghost Trio.*

"Salt-Washed Pictograph Just Beyond the Abandoned Bunker" is after Melissa Kwasny's collection *Pictograph.*

"A Permeable Membrane in the Mutable Cosmos" takes its title from *The Hungry are Dying: Beggars and Bishops in Roman Cappadocia* by Susan R. Holman, which discusses the ancient belief that eating viper meat could cure leprosy, enabling those with the disease to shed their skin like snakes do. Thank you to Jake Jacobs for making me aware of this practice.

Acknowledgments

I'm grateful to the publications in which many of the poems in this book first appeared:

Bellingham Review: "All God's Creatures Got a Place in the Choir," "Cast Your Cares Upon Him," "Self-Portrait with Cephalopod and Digitalis Purpurea," "The Windows Kept On"

Bluestem: "Concerning Nectar, Concerning Brack"

The Boiler: "Cracking the Egg," "Creation Myth"

Carve: "There Are So Many Ways to Decide What to Kill and What to Rescue," "Waking Late to a Late Spring"

Cleaver Magazine: "Poem for Trending Tragedy"

Crab Creek Review: "The Young Eat What These Birds Disgorge from their Crops"

The Collagist: "Dumb Beasts," "Most of us Aren't Beautiful, Though Some Learn How," "Spell to Turn the World Around"

Duende: "Do You Want to See More?" "A Permeable Membrane in the Mutable Cosmos"

The Gettysburg Review: "'That's Like the Oldest Trick in the Book, Next to Putting a File in the Cake,'" "Today Is the Day"

The Inlander: "What Spoils in the Sun"

Lake Effect: "Situs Inversus"

Laurel Review: "Chronic and Nameless," "Salt-Washed Pictograph Just Beyond the Abandoned Bunker"

Lilac City Fairy Tales Vol. 4: "Like Humans," "When I Stepped on the Mouths of Other Creatures, I Did Not Apologize"

Matter Monthly: "Photos of Pig That Appears to Have Blue Fat Beneath Skin Shared on Social Media"

Mid-American Review: "And the Shrill Shall Lead the Blind," "Revisiting Salt Creek"

Poetry Northwest: "Inheritance," "Of Gods and Galaxies," "Tree of Life"

Rock and Sling: "After the Funeral," "Meditation Among the Fragments," "Parable of the Sower," "Psalm Formula: Anti-epistle"

Saranac Review: "Independence Day"

Southern Indiana Review: "The Danger," "Sulfur"

Theopoetics: "Psalm Formula: Of One Afflicted," "Psalm Formula: Of the Psalmist"

Verse Wisconsin: "Perception"

WA129: An Anthology of Washington State Poets: "Legends Say"

Willow Springs: "Ode to Super Friends and Nature Television"

I'm immensely grateful to francine j. harris for selecting my manuscript for the Jake Adam York Prize, and for describing my work with the phrase "lush and obsessed and frantic and deathy," which I've now come to use anytime someone asks, "How are you?" Thank you to Wayne Miller at *Copper Nickel* and the team at Milkweed Editions for your kindness, attention, and care throughout this process.

Thank you to the friends, colleagues, teachers, fellow poets, and beloveds who guided me, these poems, and this book at every stage, especially Thom Caraway, Ben Cartwright, Linda Cooper, Jeff Dodd, Ginger Grey, Christopher Howell, Jake Jacobs, Ellie Kozlowski, Leyna Krow, Brooke Matson, Amy Munson, Kathryn Nuernberger, Laura Stott, Emily Van Kley, and Nance Van Winckel. And from the depths of my three cephalopod hearts, thank you to the Inland Jellyfish Collective—Laura Read, Ellen Welcker, and Maya Jewell Zeller. You keep my head above water. You keep me whole in this vast, calcifying tumbler.

photo: Dean Davis

KATHRYN SMITH is the author of the collection *Book of Exodus* and the chapbook *Chosen Companions of the Goblin*, winner of the 2018 Open Country Press Chapbook Contest. Her poems have appeared in *Poetry Northwest*, *Bellingham Review*, *The Journal*, *Mid-American Review*, *Redivider*, and elsewhere, and she has received an Allied Arts Foundation award, a Spokane Arts Grant Award, and a Pushcart Special Mention. She received her MFA in creative writing from Eastern Washington University and lives in Spokane, Washington, where she also makes collage and mixed media art.

milkweed
editions

Founded as a nonprofit organization in 1980,
Milkweed Editions is an independent publisher.
Our mission is to identify, nurture and publish
transformative literature, and build an engaged
community around it.

Milkweed Editions is based in Bde Ota (Minneapolis)
within Mni Sota Makoče, the traditional homeland
of the Dakota people. Residing here since time
immemorial, Dakota people still call Mni Sota
Makoče home, with four federally recognized Dakota
nations and many more Dakota people residing in
what is now the state of Minnesota. Due to continued
legacies of colonization, genocide, and forced removal,
generations of Dakota people remain disenfranchised
from their traditional homeland. Presently, Mni Sota
Makoče has become a refuge and home for many
Indigenous nations and peoples, including seven
federally recognized Ojibwe nations. We humbly
encourage readers to reflect upon the historical
legacies held in the lands they occupy.

milkweed.org

Interior design by Mary Austin Speaker
Typeset in Granjon

Granjon is a Garamond revival typeface designed
by George W. Jones in the period 1928–1929 for the
British branch of the Linotype company, based
on type cut by Claude Garamond that was used
in a book printed by Jean Poupy in 1592.